This journal belongs to:

_____

_____

_____

The WISDOM JOURNAL

"The most valuable gift you can give yourself is the time to nurture the unique spirit that is You."

—*Oprah Winfrey*

I have been journaling since I was fifteen years old.

And after looking back over hundreds of my early entries, my first *aha* is realizing that writing all of those poems in my twenties about the men who did me wrong was pretty pitiful. It's a testament to growth and grace that I've come this far.

The bigger, deeper *aha* is discovering that words matter. When they're written and not just spoken, words last forever. My journals are a form of therapy for me. Not only as I process and give thanks for what I am experiencing in the moment, but there is a profound sacredness to paging through decades-old entries to rediscover who you are, what you value, and the dreams and goals you cherish. It's astonishing to be able to track my own evolution. I recently reread my first journal from 1970, cover to cover. I laughed and cried out loud for real, and marveled at the girl I was and the woman I'm still becoming.

I know you are busy. It's the catchphrase for our time.

This is what I know to be true: Making space in your life for thoughtful reflection and journaling those thoughts is a powerful spiritual practice.

You will begin to discover what it means to actualize the truest expression of yourself. I believe that's what we're all seeking—to master our human being-ness.

At my home in Santa Barbara, there are twelve oak trees on the side of my front yard. I call them the apostles, and whenever I need clarity, I head straight for their calming canopy. There could be a hundred things on my to-do list, but if I'm under the oaks, those trees remind me how to be: still. This is the spot where I most love to journal. Create your own sacred space. Is it a back porch or a bathtub for you? A window seat or your favorite chair?

Being aware of the space that speaks to you is important. Surround yourself in the comfort and resonance that bring you the most joy, open your journal, and begin to express all that you hold within your heart.

Your life is calling!

—*Oprah*

"The perfect moment
is this one."

—Jon Kabat-Zinn

"Any day you learn a
lesson is a great day."

—*Tracey Jackson*

"Silence is the one spiritual discipline that is found in all world religions."

—*Father Richard Rohr*

"Your life is always
speaking to you.
The fundamental
spiritual question is:
Will you listen?"

—Oprah Winfrey

"Never lose sight of the horizon, even though in this moment you are not seeing it."

—Mark Nepo

"I try to live my life knowing if you can see it, feel it, and believe it, then you can achieve it."

—*Amy Purdy*

"Find a way!"

—*Diana Nyad*

"The secret to finding your passion is to start bringing passion to everything you do."

—*Marie Forleo*

"Intention is the why
beneath the why."

—*Gary Zukav*

"You can't get to courage without walking through vulnerability."

—*Brené Brown*

"Life is too short to suffer."

—*Tony Robbins*

"The soul often
speaks through
longing."

—Sue Monk Kidd

"Our deepest fear is not that we are inadequate. Our deepest fear is that we are powerful beyond measure."

—*Marianne Williamson*

"Am I living a life
that I can admire?"

—*Diana Nyad*

"I looked around thinking I wanted to be like all those people in lights, and I found myself happiest in places nobody wanted to be."

—*Timothy Shriver*

"When your
personality comes
to serve the
energy of the soul,
that is authentic
empowerment."

—*Gary Zukav*

"What follows 'I am'
we're inviting into
our life."

—*Pastor Joel Osteen*

"The ego can't exist
in consciousness."

—*Eckhart Tolle*

"If you don't raise
yourself first, and
parent yourself, then
you will aspire to
make your child
a mini version of
yourself."

—*Dr. Shefali Tsabary*

"You can accept
or reject the way
you are treated by
others, but until you
heal the wounds of
your past, you will
continue to bleed."

—Iyanla Vanzant

"Give yourself permission to let go of the past and step out of your history into the now!"

—Oprah Winfrey

"Pay attention to the assignments that are coming to you, and show up for them! Everything comes up so it can be healed."

—*Gabrielle Bernstein*

"Every time we are negative about someone we are actually affecting ourselves."

—Jack Canfield

"Take responsibility
for the energy you
bring into this
space."

—Dr. Jill Bolte Taylor

"You can't get mercy
unless you give it."

—*Bryan Stevenson*

"We sin when we
 have our loves out
 of order."

—*Saint Augustine*

"Everybody tells
the truth with
something."

—*Glennon Doyle*

"The truth will set
you free, but you
have to endure
the labor pains of
birthing it."

—Iyanla Vanzant

"I'm going through a very hard time. I'm not going to waste this precious experience, this opportunity to become the best me."

—*Elizabeth Lesser*

"Trust is knowing
there is a power
greater than yourself
at work here. And
trusting it will all
work out."

—*Tracey Jackson*

"I would rather flirt with failure than never dance with my joy."

—*Wes Moore*

"Gratefulness is the experience of the great fullness of life."

—*Brother David Steindl-Rast*

"An audience moving together on a belly laugh, that's praying, that's gratitude, that's enjoyment."

—Norman Lear

"What if we woke up
in the morning and
were so grateful for
the sweet territory of
silence and sleep?"

—*Lynne Twist*

"If the only prayer
you say in your
entire life is thank
you, that will be
enough."

—*Meister Eckhart*

"Grace is a power
that comes in
and transforms
a moment to
something better."

—*Caroline Myss*

"Humanity is the ability to hurt for others. You must know people as people, and you must do what they need in the middle of their pain."

—*Sister Joan Chittister*

"Use your life to serve the world and you will discover the myriad ways the world offers itself to serve you."

—*Oprah Winfrey*

"Love is when what you want is never important, but what the other person needs and wants is always paramount."

—*Pastor Wintley Phipps*

FLATIRON
BOOKS
NEW YORK

For information, address Flatiron Books, 175 Fifth Avenue, New York, NY 10010.
www.flatironbooks.com

Our books may be purchased in bulk for promotional, educational, or business use. Please contact
your local bookseller or the Macmillan Corporate and Premium Sales Department at 1-800-221-7945,
extension 5442, or by e-mail at MacmillanSpecialMarkets@macmillan.com.

Library of Congress Cataloging-in-Publication Data is available upon request.

ISBN: 978-1-250-19765-8

MELCHER
MEDIA

Produced by Melcher Media
124 West 13th Street
New York, NY 10011
www.melcher.com

President and CEO: Charles Melcher
Vice President and COO: Bonnie Eldon
Executive Editor/Producer: Lauren Nathan
Senior Editor/Producer: Aaron Kenedi
Production Director: Susan Lynch
Senior Digital Producer: Shannon Fanuko

Contributing editorial: Jenna Kostelnik Utley
Cover design: Grace Yoon
Interior design: Renee Bollier
Cover photograph: Melissa Gidney Daly

First Edition: October 2017

10 9 8 7 6 5 4 3 2